Ever
Insights

Self-Acceptance

Rosalyn Derges

CWR

Dedication

In order to have been able to write this devotional, I have been blessed by the invaluable input I have received from the various ministries at CWR.

This journey toward self-acceptance began with the Counselling Certificate course with Angie Coombes and Elaine Baker, who taught me so much about being fully accepted and approved of by God. Later, I became a part of the Introduction to Christian Care and Counselling team, with Angie as well as Richard Laws, where I grew in confidence as I taught on being free to be who we are because we know that we are loved, valued and have worth in God's heart. The CWR Inspiring Women team, with Lynette Brooks, Lynne Penson and Rosie Morgan, has continued to be a place of growth in my spiritual journey, and writing for other CWR publications has added to my understanding of the value of self-acceptance.

Thank you to you all. It has been a life-changing experience and a joy to my heart.

Introduction

As I come to write this devotional, I am acutely aware that my own self-acceptance muscles have yet to be further developed. My journey through counselling training, teaching the importance of self-awareness and writing previous devotionals has definitely taught me the value of accepting myself. I am certainly further along the road than I used to be!

How do we define ourselves? In what ways do we allow the words of others to define who we are? Is our concept of self-acceptance based on what others think or what God says about us? The old saying 'Sticks and stones may break my bones, but words will never hurt me' could not be less true. Our hearts are tender and can undoubtedly be hurt and even broken by careless, negative words. Our self-acceptance, if based on those negative experiences, will not be truly healthy. I have discovered that exploring this issue is not self-indulgent, but is releasing and restorative. It leads to a freedom that will enable us to enjoy the fullness of life Jesus promised.

My prayer for us as we study this important area of our lives is that we will be blessed, encouraged and equipped with the truth in God's

Word about our value to Him and that we are created as His masterpiece. May we grasp that, as a perfect Father, He made us in His image and therefore we are acceptable to Him. The problem is that we have developed negative thinking and behaviours that need to be adjusted. But God, because of His deep love for us, will walk with us as we learn to accept ourselves.

Growth and development towards maturity has always been a longing of my heart, so thank you for joining me as we explore how to become more accepting of ourselves, along with a greater awareness of the Father's love and acceptance of each one of us. One of the ways we can become more mindful of this is by reading and coming into agreement with His holy Word – something we will look at together throughout this devotional.

God knows everything about me

READ: PSALM 139:1–12

'You have searched me, LORD, and you know me.' (v1)

Does the fact that God sees into every part of our being, and is aware of our every movement, encourage you or make you feel uneasy? He has an intimate knowledge of our thoughts. How does that make you feel? The psalmist, David, obviously saw it as positive. David's awareness that God knows him so well breathed life into his relationship with God and made clear to him God's presence: 'You go before me and follow me'; and God's blessing: 'You place your hand of blessing on my head' (v5, NLT).

Wherever David went, he was secure in the knowledge that God would guide him, strengthen him and support him. He clearly accepted that he was loved by the Father in spite of his own failings. And this is often our challenge with self-acceptance. We are so acutely aware of our failings and can often feel unlovable; we wouldn't want others to know what goes on in every part of our lives, let alone our minds!

Self-acceptance is an attitude that says, 'I know I'm not perfect. This is how I am at the moment

– and it's OK'. It is about taking responsibility for ourselves in both our strengths and weaknesses. Self-respect acknowledges that we make mistakes but has an attitude of learning from them and moving forward. Sometimes, though, we may tend to rehearse our mistakes and come up with negative self-talk that can affect our self-esteem.

When we can accept where we are in life and walk in confidence, we experience a sense of ease within. In Psalm 131:2, King David says: 'I have calmed and quietened myself... I am content.' How can we find this state of restfulness? Here are some keys I have found helpful: 1. Refuse to live in fear. Watch your language of fear; saying 'I dread it when...' sets us up for negativity. 2. Be led by the Spirit. Choose each day to ask God's Spirit to go with you. 3. Be intentional in facing the day. Know what steals your joy and recognise the joy given by Jesus. 4. Keep a good balance. Glorifying the concept of being busy can leave us burnt out and stressed. 5. Enjoy being who you are. Having unrealistic expectations of ourselves or others leads to dissatisfaction and unease.

Father, as I begin focusing on my attitude toward self-acceptance, help me to gain a balanced view of how You see me, and how I then see myself in the light of Your amazing presence in my life. Amen.

God has created me

READ: PSALM 139:13–18

'I praise you because I am fearfully and wonderfully made' (v14)

When we look at the airbrushed, 'perfect' bodies and faces of celebrities all over the media, we can certainly feel challenged! We may feel we are overweight or too thin, too short or too tall. Maybe we are conscious of our hair growth or the way our neck looks. Whatever our perceived physical issue, the truth is: we are, indeed, fearfully and wonderfully made. The human body is a miraculous work of art and so brilliantly complex. But our perception of it, if negative, can affect our self-acceptance.

We are so much more than our physical bodies though. We have a mind, emotions and the ability to make choices – as well as a spirit that is filled with the Spirit of God. The beautiful words of this psalm encourage us to be thankful for how we are made and how much we are thought of in the heart of the Father: 'How precious to me are your thoughts, God! How vast is the sum of them!

Were I to count them, they would outnumber the grains of sand – when I awake, I am still with you' (vv17–18).

Knowing we are precious to God, that He created us in His image, that He thinks about us continually, can increase our confidence in who we are. It's important for us to understand God as a God of love and power – one who protects, is faithful, kind and consistent in every way. A.W. Tozer said: 'We can never know who or what we are till we know at least something of what God is.' God created us with a longing to be loved by Him, to be dependent on Him, and when we are, our self-respect and acceptance grows. In fact, what happens is that we come into agreement with what our Father thinks about us.

Read this psalm again, as a prayer from your heart to His. And if you can't quite believe it yet, pray in faith, letting the words filter into your mind and heart.

Lord, help me to understand more fully how much I am known by You. I am part of Your creation and You have made all things well. Teach me how to depend on You more. Lay Your hand of blessing on me and keep me close to You. Amen.

Experience God's peace

READ: PHILIPPIANS 4:4–7

'Do not be anxious about anything, but in every situation, by prayer and petition, with thanksgiving, present your requests to God.' (v6)

We have said that we have been created in God's image. We have seen that He is someone who thinks, and amazingly thinks about us all the time. But He also feels, chooses and is Spirit. Therefore, we can call ourselves thinking, emotional, choosing and spiritual beings. However, some, if not all, of these characteristics can be distorted. Because of our experiences and how we perceive them, our thinking, our emotions and therefore our behaviour can leave us far from peaceful. But in this passage, we have guidelines for a peaceful life. And a life at peace builds our sense of self-acceptance.

The mind is something that can take us down a dark road of negative thinking and can certainly affect our emotions and self-esteem. The challenges that life can bring require us to think deeply when we make decisions about how to respond, and sometimes we don't respond well, especially if we are led by our emotions. They are not always reliable, and they can be quite powerful – but they are not *wrong*. Emotions tell us what is going on within and it is important to recognise them, accept them and manage them well. It may help to take a few moments, when they rise up, to ask yourself what you are feeling and why, and then decide what you are going to do with them. I have found that this has really helped me to slow down and take stock rather than react negatively out of those emotions.

So, what are the guidelines for peace here? The New Living Translation puts it this way: 'Always be full of joy in the Lord. I say it again— rejoice! Let everyone see that you are considerate in all you do. Remember, the Lord is coming soon. Don't worry about anything; instead, pray about everything. Tell God what you need, and thank him for all he has done. Then you will experience God's peace, which exceeds anything we can understand. His peace will guard your hearts and minds as you live in Christ Jesus.'

Lord, I choose to be full of joy in You. Let me see that You are with me every day. I choose not to worry; instead I will pray. I will tell You what I need and thank You for what You have done. May I experience Your unexplainable peace. Amen.

You are part of it!

READ: 1 CORINTHIANS 12:12–27

'Now you are the body of Christ, and each one of you is a part of it.' (v27)

For many years I was involved in counselling ministry and, in that time, I saw that many people were not at ease with their personalities and abilities. There was a tendency for people to compare themselves with others and see those others as better, more able or more appealing. When we evaluate ourselves in that way, our self-acceptance gets knocked out of balance. We begin to devalue how we are made and see our personality, gifts and abilities as lesser. These words from Corinthians clearly show that everyone has value in God's kingdom, and each is made different for a purpose.

Isabel Briggs Myers, who with her mother created a personality type indicator to help people understand themselves better, wrote: 'The best-adjusted people are the "psychologically patriotic," who are glad to be what they are.'[1] I once worked in a school setting with a group of teenagers who were exhibiting low self-esteem even though they were intelligent and wonderful people. It quickly became evident that they saw their more extraverted peers as brighter and more successful than themselves. Their gentle introvert personalities meant they didn't contribute so much in class discussions, which left them feeling low in confidence. To help them, I encouraged them to voice their appreciation of one another, sharing the positive attributes each had. Then I explained the value of a personality with a preference for introversion, and the importance of celebrating how we are made. Introverts generally need time to process information and will respond with valuable input when given that time. I later heard that this group began to grow in confidence as they supported one another.

Verse 18 of this passage says, 'But in fact God has placed the parts in the body [God's kingdom], every one of them, just as he wanted them to be.' God created us with different personalities and abilities so we could use them, develop them, appreciate them and accept them as gifts from His hand.

Father, thank You for the abilities You have gifted me with. Help me to see how I can best use them for Your purposes. Help me to understand my personality and accept how You have created me. Amen.

Jesus is loved

READ: MATTHEW 3:13–17

'And a voice from heaven said, "This is my Son, whom I love; with him I am well pleased."' (v17)

We are going to spend the next three days considering the concept of Jesus' own self-acceptance. He is our model, as we are encouraged to become more like Him. These few verses describe both a public yet intimate moment between the Father and the Son. Jesus knows He is loved so He is completely secure in who He is.

We can see that though He is the creator of the universe, Jesus humbles Himself before His cousin John to be baptised. John recognises the perfection and holiness of Jesus and is at first reluctant to baptise Him, but Jesus is committed to being obedient to His Father's will and insists on it. Then comes the beautiful moment when heaven opens up, the Spirit descends like a dove and the Father speaks those words of affirmation and love.

Part of self-acceptance is about knowing we are secure, we belong and we are loved.

When we only try to find that sense of security in relationships, possessions, the workplace, wealth, looks or other transient things, we can be bitterly disappointed. Jesus' trust in His Father enabled Him to act in both humility and power; in vulnerability and strength. Whenever He was pushed, berated or challenged, Jesus acted and responded from a place of security. I love that about Him, and it is an area I want to continue to grow in. Jesus cared about everyone, but He was not prepared to dance to their tune if it was out of sync with God's will. His Father's love was His strongest motivator, not only for His behaviour but also how He thought about Himself.

In John 15:9 Jesus tells us, 'As the Father has loved me, so have I loved you.' This love bond between Father and Son is available to us also. We too can find that place of security and belonging in God. Jesus accepted His place in the Father's heart – will we?

Father, help me to consider and understand more deeply the unconditional place I have in Your heart. Amen.

Jesus understood His value

READ: LUKE 4:14–21

'The Spirit of the Lord is on me, because
he has anointed me to proclaim
good news' (v18)

Jesus had a clear understanding of His purpose
on earth, and He declared it in the Temple in His
childhood town of Nazareth at the beginning of
His public ministry. Having recently returned
from the wilderness, where He had been tempted
by the devil, He was full of the Holy Spirit and
ready to teach the truth and help people to
understand the love, power and authority of God
in a way they had never heard or understood
before. At first, He was praised by everyone
because of His words of wisdom and clarity of
understanding. However, when He shared that
part of His purpose was to spread the good news
further afield – to foreigners and strangers – the
people became incensed and tried to harm Him.

Another part of self-acceptance is knowing,
understanding and embracing our purpose in
life. Jesus modelled this ability perfectly. He set
His heart in the direction His Father called Him
to and never wavered – even when death stared

Him in the face. Reminding ourselves of the illustration of 'the body', we can see that there are so many different ways in which we can use our abilities. When we bring joy and devotion to whatever God has gifted us with, it blesses others and gives us a sense of wellbeing. One business coach is said to ask himself at the end of each day, 'Who have I added value to today?' When we discover and appreciate the purpose we have been called to, whatever that role might be, we add value to others. As Max Lucado writes: 'Remember, no one else has your talents. No one. God elevates you from common-hood by matching your unique abilities to custom-made assignments.'[2]

Jesus came to fulfil a purpose. He accepted it and gave it His all. We are also designed to fulfil a purpose, humbly accepting that however 'elevated' it may appear to be it brings glory to our Lord. Some of us may need to begin that journey of self-discovery; others may need to develop and hone the skills we have; and others may need to redefine what we do to match our unique abilities to our 'custom-made assignments'.

Father, You created me, enabled me and blessed me with abilities. Now empower me to fulfil what You are calling me to for Your glory. Amen.

He is the Way

READ: JOHN 14:6–7

'I am the way and the truth and the life.' (v6)

While some might have seen Jesus as arrogant and full of pride, there was nothing wrong with His self-worth! He was completely self-assured because He understood His value both to God and humanity. Jesus described Himself as the way, the truth, the life, the bread of life, the light of the world, the good shepherd, the gate for the sheep, God's Son, the resurrection and the life, the true vine. This is a man who knows His worth. His honesty and self-awareness teaches us something about the importance of knowing who we are in God, appreciating it, acknowledging it and accepting it with an open heart and mind.

Our value to God is comparable to the value He places in Jesus, because Jesus' life was given in redemption for ours. And that is truly awesome! It seems to make sense, then, that we learn to embrace the truth of what God says about us in His Word. We are completely loved (Eph. 1:7–9); we are His workmanship, His masterpiece, His work of art (Eph. 2:10); we have been given eternal life (Eph. 2:4–6); we have an inheritance (Eph. 1:14); we are God's sons and daughters (Rom. 8:15). Sometimes we can have a slave mentality where we don't feel we deserve to live as sons and daughters of the King of kings, but Jesus died to give us that privilege, and that is our value and worth to Him.

A child of God who has a balanced sense of self-acceptance receives this truth and lives from a place of deep assurance that in spite of any imperfections, mistakes made, less than appropriate behaviours and words spoken in haste, they are magnificently embraced by a loving God who accepts them as they are and gently encourages them to become more like Jesus.

Spend some time considering what the Bible says about who you are in God as a son or daughter. Ask Him what characteristic He would like you to more fully accept, and let His Spirit grow that in you.

Lord, forgive me for not fully taking hold of the truth that I am of great value to You. May my sense of self-worth increase as I meditate on Your words of love for me. Amen.

Jesus knows

READ: JOHN 21:15–17

'He said, "Lord, you know all things; you know that I love you."' (v17)

I wonder if, out of fear, shame or concern of what others think of us, we may have hidden the truth and even lied to protect ourselves. Peter had previously been in a very difficult situation, and in the heat of the moment he denied Jesus to safeguard himself (see Luke 22:54–62). Almost immediately, though, Peter deeply regretted it and was distraught. I wonder, too, if he might have wrestled with that denial and found himself overwhelmed with guilt and shame, unable to accept himself because what he had done had lodged a negative self-image deep in his mind. Peter had such a strong desire to follow and support Jesus, he found it hard to believe that he would ever betray Him. But under intense pressure, he had cracked and broken his own rule of 'I will never...'

Shame is an enemy of self-respect. In their book on self-acceptance, Chris Ledger and Claire Musters write: 'Shame drives us to keep our pain hidden for fear of judgment... Shame is a part of ourselves that we hate and want to keep hidden, even from ourselves.' When we push our feelings down in this way and we bury them alive, they still have the power to cause us to lose self-esteem, peace of mind and heart, as well as self-acceptance. When we behave in ways that disappoint us, we can often harshly judge or even condemn ourselves.

This is where Jesus was magnificent towards Peter. He knew the agony of heart he had experienced, and wanted to give him an opportunity to receive healing and wholeness. Jesus asked Peter three times if he loved Him – once wasn't enough. With each question, Jesus released him from his guilt and set him free. Before this life-changing conversation, Peter was prepared to go back to being a fisherman, but Jesus had other plans. He had a role for Peter that meant he needed to walk out of a place of shame and into a place of freedom. Peter needed to know who he was in Christ.

Jesus offers us the same freedom, and together we will explore this further.

Thank You, Lord, that You know all things. You know my heart and mind, and You know the things I have hidden away. Help me to find that place of freedom in You. Amen.

Radically transformed

READ: 1 TIMOTHY 1:12–17

'The grace of our Lord was poured out on me abundantly, along with the faith and love that are in Christ Jesus.' (v14)

Before he became an apostle, Paul (then called Saul) had persecuted the Church with vengeance. He often mentioned his past life in his epistles, as he does here in 1 Timothy. His life and attitude is an amazing example of how the love of Jesus can radically transform our own lives. Paul's testimony is incredible. He was able to walk in the freedom Christ's death and resurrection bought for him without allowing feelings of shame to rob him of his joy or get in the way of him fulfilling the purpose for which God had called him.

As we read these words from 1 Timothy, we see that Paul was aware of God's strength to enable him; believed God considered him to be trustworthy; recognised he was appointed by God to serve; knew he had received God's mercy; believed God filled him with faith and love. He was, in effect, saying that if *he* received all of this, anyone can – no matter what they have done.

What enabled Paul to so quickly move from

persecuting the Church to encouraging people to become part of it? He met Jesus in a powerful way. In Acts 9 we read the account of his encounter with Jesus, during which he was overwhelmed by the light from heaven, was made blind for three days, was met and counselled by Ananias, and was prayed for to be filled with the Holy Spirit. Scales fell from Paul's eyes so he could see, and he was baptised. He spent time in the company of the believers for a few days, and then obediently followed the Lord into his ministry!

I believe there are three things here that we can learn from. Firstly, Paul was filled with the Spirit. God's Spirit is a powerful comforter who enables us to know who we are in Christ Jesus. Secondly, Paul spent time in the company of believers who supported him. God's intention is for us to be part of a support network of mature believers. Thirdly, Paul didn't let his past hold him back. God does not want us to remain in a place of self-condemnation; He paid a high price to release us from that.

Holy God, help me to see that there is nothing I can do to stop You from loving and accepting me. Help me to receive the comfort of Your Spirit, the counsel of godly people, and to move out of a place of self-condemnation. Amen.

God is fair

READ: ROMANS 3:21–30

'Yet God, in his grace, freely makes us right in his sight. He did this through Christ Jesus when he freed us from the penalty for our sins.' (v24, NLT)

We have seen that Paul, knowing what his past was like, accepted that he got it terribly wrong. He described himself as the worst of sinners, but because of God's mercy he was forgiven, and was able to accept it and move forward. Paul's declaration of the character of God in these verses clearly shows that God is fair, full of grace and righteousness, and has a forgiving heart. This was the theme of his ministry because he himself was assured of it in his own life.

We can so easily feel unworthy when we allow our past or troubling thoughts to dictate who we are. An over-sensitive conscience can keep us in a place of false guilt where we can experience personal blame and distress. God has created us with a conscience to protect us and guide us to make right choices, but an overly vulnerable conscience is an inaccurate guide. In the past, I have tended to replay things I have said and done over and over in my mind, to the point that they took me down a dark road of very negative thinking. Although I accepted how much I was loved by God, I found it difficult to love and accept myself when I believed I had made mistakes.

What I began to realise is that my thought life was not lining up with how God thought about me. Paul clearly demonstrates the power of coming into agreement with God's Word by placing our faith in Jesus who has redeemed every part of who we are – including our minds! In Romans 8:1–2, Paul writes something that, for me, was hugely significant: 'So now there is no condemnation for those who belong to Christ Jesus. And because you belong to him, the power of the life-giving Spirit has freed you from the power of sin that leads to death' (NLT). With Christ's redemptive power, along with the Holy Spirit's life-giving power, we have everything we need to overcome what might sabotage our living in freedom. How amazing is that?

Lord, You have the life-giving power to release me from darkness and bring me into the light of Your forgiving and loving heart. Help me to accept that truth as I put my faith in You. Amen.

Behaving badly

READ: 2 SAMUEL 11:1–17; PSALM 51:7

'Cleanse me with hyssop, and I shall be clean; wash me, and I shall be whiter than snow.' (Psa. 51:7)

When David was faced with the force of King Saul's personal attacks and wrong attitude, he had immense self-control and displayed honourable behaviour. His men were amazed at his restraint, especially when he could have so easily overcome Saul (see 1 Sam. 24). But when it came to the temptation of a relationship with Bathsheba, he was unable to resist such a beautiful woman. His behaviour throughout this incident in his life was, quite frankly, appalling. He had hoped he could keep what he had done a secret from Uriah, but Uriah's principled behaviour moved David towards a shameful and callous act. What David had hoped to cover up, God was fully aware of and was not about to let him off the hook.

In 2 Samuel 12 we read that God used Nathan the prophet to confront David with what he had done. He wanted to bring it out into the open, so David had to face his crime. When David was confronted by the truth, he was full of remorse and confessed his sin. Then Nathan told him he was already forgiven, though there would be rebellion in his family and this child with Bathsheba would die. David immediately prayed, fasted and pleaded with God to spare the child, but while he was forgiven, he still faced the tragic consequences of what he had done. What happened then confused his advisors: King David refreshed himself and went into the Tabernacle to worship God. He wasn't prepared to let this episode hold him back or stop him from worshipping.

It seems that when there was still hope that God would change His mind, David humbled himself before Him, agonising over what he had done. When it was over, he acknowledged God's authority and accepted His sovereignty in this matter.

In Psalm 51, a psalm David wrote about his feelings after this event, he asked God to cleanse him with hyssop (hyssop is a herb used for medicinal purposes as well as internal purification) and wash him so he could be made pure again. God's forgiveness and purification was paramount to his moving on with his life, not wallowing in self-pity or lack of self-forgiveness.

Father, Your forgiveness releases healing. Your cleansing restores my inner being. I praise You. Amen.

I am forgiven

READ: PSALM 51

'My sacrifice, O God, is a broken spirit; a broken and contrite heart you, God, will not despise.' (v17)

In this psalm, David sets out before God his remorse at what he has done. He asks God for mercy and forgiveness, knowing this is the only way he will be able to be released from an agonising guilt. David asks to be purified and for God to create a clean heart within him, renewing his spirit. I would suggest that because of his worshipful attitude and relationship with God, David has a clear sense of what God is looking for in his heart. He longs for God's salvation: 'Restore to me the joy of your salvation and grant me a willing spirit, to sustain me' (v12).

Healthy guilt about things we may have done or not done moves us to make restoration and re-establishes a sense of peace within. Unhealthy guilt can be like a crippling prison of condemnation and torment. Our conscience, if guilt is not dealt with, can lead us towards internal suffering that keeps us bound and certainly affects our self-acceptance. David's way of dealing with guilt in this psalm is a helpful process we may do well to emulate: ask God for mercy, acknowledging His love; ask Him to cleanse and purify; recognise and acknowledge the fault; ask God to restore and renew what is good; ask for forgiveness; decide to worship and come to a place of wholeness.

The keys to walking free from guilt are accepting the fact that God has already forgiven us out of His amazing heart of love, and accepting the need to forgive ourselves. C.S. Lewis wrote, 'I think that if God forgives us, we must forgive ourselves. Otherwise it is almost like setting up ourselves as a higher tribunal than Him.'[3]

Do you forgive yourself? Whatever we have done in the past has been entirely cleansed and we are purified by the blood of Jesus. God loves us too much to leave us in a state of sin. Like David, though, in order to be free to worship God and acknowledge His sovereignty in our lives, we need to *accept* this incredible gift of forgiveness and, therefore, life.

Loving, forgiving God, thank You for Your mercy. Thank You that I can come to You and know You do not reject a broken and contrite heart. Amen.

●13

Accepted!

READ: LUKE 15:11–22

'But while he was still a long way off, his father saw him and was filled with compassion for him; he ran to his son, threw his arms round him and kissed him.' (v20)

God created you because He wanted you. He gave you abilities and talents because He has a plan for your life. He sent Jesus to die for you because He didn't want you to be burdened by having to earn your way to heaven – it is a gift! Quite often, in our effort to please people and perform well, we try to be perfect, setting ourselves high standards we may not always be able to fulfil. We are unable to accept ourselves as we are and may even start to feel empty and worthless. The prodigal son came to such a place as he looked at the reality of his life and saw what it had become.

In this story, Jesus was explaining that however far you feel from God's presence, whoever you are and whatever your background has been, you are welcome to run into His arms and be accepted, loved, forgiven and restored. Not only was the son enveloped in his father's embrace, he was given significant items to re-establish his position. The robe proved his identity as a son; the ring was a family seal that gave him the authority to work in his father's business; the shoes denoted he was a family member and not a slave; the party proclaimed that the father was thrilled to have his son back and was not ashamed of him.

It would have made no sense if the son turned around and said, 'I cannot accept these things – I don't deserve them', and then walked away. When we live in the acceptance of the Father heart of God, we are in a spacious place where, even though we make mistakes, we can experience an unconditional belonging and sense of value, which frees us. How fantastic is that? Jesus is giving us full permission here to live freely and abundantly in this place of acceptance. In order to come into agreement with that, we need to fully accept ourselves as children of the King.

Lord, I pray that I will receive my identity as Your child, the seal of authority to fulfil my role in Your kingdom, and the knowledge that I belong in Your family. Help me to accept that You are overjoyed to embrace me. Amen.

Go in peace

READ: LUKE 7:36–50

'Therefore, I tell you, her many sins have been forgiven – as her great love has shown. But whoever has been forgiven little loves little.' (v47)

What makes you frustrated or angry? I get annoyed when people behind me in a queue for a supermarket till get to go to the newly opened checkout ahead of me. It doesn't seem fair. I also tend to get frustrated at drivers who are so cautious they drive slowly and hold me up. It can get tedious! What about you? Perhaps your tendency is to become easily anxious or even fearful in certain situations, causing you to hold back and not get involved. Or do you push through and 'just do it' afraid?

Emotions can so easily drive us into doing or saying things we later regret, or prevent us from fully achieving our goals. In our reading today, the woman who anointed Jesus' feet must have pushed through any fear she may have had of being judged, because her desire to bless the Lord and declare her adoration for Him outshone that fear. The Pharisee's judgment of her as a sinner didn't sabotage her act of love; she stuck around. We might easily have been part of the condemnation group, believing the perfume could have been put to better use, piously suggesting it might have been used to feed the poor. But were their reactions indicating what they thought Jesus wanted to hear? Did they think He would have congratulated them on their virtuous thinking? They got it so very wrong.

Jesus understood this woman's heart and what she was trying to say by doing what she did. Her act of contrition completely freed her from her sins, and Jesus said she had many. I wonder if when she entered the house she was bowed down with guilt, but when she left she was lifted in freedom and peace.

Here Jesus showed how completely accepting He is. He accepted the woman's loving act without embarrassment and challenged the Pharisees without fear. In order to fully accept ourselves as we are, we need to recognise and moderate any inclination towards angry, fearful or judgmental reactions; and instead, humble ourselves before God in worship, letting Him heal and deliver us from sinful behaviour.

You are wonderful, Lord Jesus. I worship You with all my heart. Amen.

Be careful how you think

READ: 1 KINGS 19:1–13; PROVERBS 4:23

'Above all else, guard your heart, for everything you do flows from it.' (Prov. 4:23)

The Good News Translation puts the above verse this way: 'Be careful how you think; your life is shaped by your thoughts.' This is so true and we are wise to take notice of it. What is your thought life like? How does it shape the rest of your life?

We have an inner voice that can either be critical or encouraging. Unfortunately, our critical voice often shouts louder than our encouraging one. We may even find that the inner critical voice is protecting our vulnerability. As a child, I experienced some negative reactions from other children, leading to me being alienated from my peer group. Over the years, I told myself that others probably would not want to be my friend. That inner voice protected me from more hurt by saying, 'If you don't get involved in that group of friends, you won't be rejected – so stay safe.' This inner critical voice, though meaning well, can often grow in us and cause the negativity to be unregulated.[4] We can sometimes chew a thought over until it causes us to feel negatively about ourselves, even to the point of depression.

That's what happened to Elijah. He had been in a situation of great triumph when God used him to overwhelm the prophets of Baal with the contest at Mount Carmel (see 1 Kings 18). When Jezebel heard, she was enraged and sent him a message saying she was going to kill him. Elijah was terrified. He was also feeling threatened by the thought that he was the only living prophet of God left: "'I have had enough, Lord,' he said. "Take my life; I am no better than my ancestors'" (v4). He was fearful, his self-esteem was low, his mood had plummeted, and he was exhausted. It was his thinking and his perspective that could have destroyed him – but God stepped in.

Practically, God sent an angel to give Elijah food and drink; he rested, ate again and then went to the mountain of the Lord, where he heard the voice of God whispering to him. Rest, nourishment and the gentle voice of God did it for Elijah. When our thinking is out of control, we might need to check our need for rest, the quality of our nourishment, and come to God for that gentle whisper of encouragement.

Mighty God, I invite You to step in when my thinking is out of control. Whisper into my soul Your words of encouragement. Amen.

The war in my mind

READ: ROMANS 7:21–8:2

'but I see another law at work in me, waging war against the law of my mind and making me a prisoner of the law of sin at work within me.' (7:23)

Growing up, I believed I was not very clever. I looked around at my classmates and noticed how well they did in comparison to me. My exam results were not great, and I struggled with understanding some of the subjects on the curriculum. Looking back now, I realise that the way I was taught just didn't match my style of learning. The consequence of this was that my self-acceptance has been slow to develop. This belief shaped my early life with a lack of confidence, a decision to stick to what I knew, a struggle to accept myself when I got things wrong and a heightened awareness of what others might be thinking about me.

The battle we have in our thinking is not so much about the actual experiences we have or the actions of others; it is fed by the mind that gives these significance. Paul's experience and behaviour, as we have seen, had to be overcome with his desire to serve God with all his heart. These verses show that he occasionally struggled with his mind – it was like a war zone for him. His comfort and answer, he writes, is Jesus Christ our Lord. And again, we consider this wonderful verse, which is certainly something we need our minds to dwell on: 'Therefore, there is now no condemnation for those who are in Christ Jesus' (8:1). When we deliberately focus on the saving power of Jesus' love and acceptance, our thinking can be changed. Paul goes on: 'because through Christ Jesus the law of the Spirit who gives life has set you free from the law of sin and death' (8:2).

The truth is, we will need to constantly come back to that place of being filled with the love and acceptance of Jesus. Our minds are very powerful and can take us back down the wrong road. Like learning a new skill, we have to keep practising new, godly thinking. When I find myself being challenged by negative thinking, I remind myself who I am in Jesus, and remember I have moved on and am no longer a child at school but a child of God, and one who is not condemned. That is so liberating!

Lord Jesus, in You I am free. May my mind focus on that truth each day. Amen.

Who am I?

READ: EXODUS 3:1–14

'But Moses said to God, "Who am I that I should go to Pharaoh and bring the Israelites out of Egypt?"' (v11)

Moses was called a friend of God, and he had the remarkable task of leading over a million people out of slavery and into freedom. He had to face the might of an Egyptian Pharaoh and was challenged by the complaints of a grumbling nation. What a job! And yet, when God first called him, Moses believed he wasn't up to the task. He felt unqualified, unknown, that he wouldn't be believed, and ill-equipped. Finally, he pleaded with God to send someone else (Exod. 4:13). Poor guy – what a daunting commission he had been given!

When God calls, He equips, but we might have trouble believing that. Moses certainly did. When God told Moses to say, 'I AM has sent me to you', He was declaring that Moses had all the power of heaven behind him; that the everlasting God was in control of what was about to happen. Our own assignment in life may not seem as epic as Moses' mission, nevertheless that same mighty God is with us in whatever we are called to do. And that gives strength to our work, inner being and mind.

I don't know about you, but when I sense God calling me to something new, I can begin to make all kinds of excuses about my inability and lack of experience. Often, though, He brings alongside us someone to support us, just as He did when He suggested Aaron could go with Moses. We also have the Holy Spirit as our guide and comforter – He is with us in every way to support, strengthen and give us the capacity to fulfil that assignment. But the Holy Spirit is with us in the everyday stuff too: our relationships, our job, our family life with all that entails. He is with us in our sense of self, helping us with the struggles we may be having.

God through His Spirit knows us, believes in us, qualifies us, and equips us. Self-acceptance means we believe this to be true and can begin to embrace each day with the attitude that we are not alone, but that the great I AM is walking with us.

Holy Spirit, I pray You will support me, comfort me and guide me through each day. Thank You that I am known, believed in, qualified and equipped to fulfil the plan You have for me. Amen.

'I must', 'I ought', 'I should'

READ: LUKE 15:25–32

'"My son," the father said, "you are always with me, and everything I have is yours."' (v31)

We return to the story of the prodigal son, but this time focusing on the older son. It is fairly obvious what his thinking has done to his mood, reactions and relationships. Right now he is angry, hurt, and feels he has been unfairly treated. He has been working hard to prove his worth, and striving for what the father could give him. On the outside, he wants to do everything right. But his heart is hardened. Jesus' picture of the older son was referring to the Pharisees who tried to earn their way into God's heart by keeping the law and doing things 'right'. They tended to be judgmental and were against Jesus' acceptance of tax collectors and sinners.

It is possible the older son's internal scripts and rules made him believe he wasn't accepted for who he was but for what he could do. This is not God's way or His desire for us. What we believe influences what we think and how we behave. In our childhood years, we are great observers but poor interpreters, which means that as we grow, we observe what makes the people in our lives happy or unhappy. Subsequently, we behave in ways that enable us to feel accepted. As a result of this, we come to develop internal rules to adhere to.[5]

It's likely that the older son set his inner script around the frame of 'working hard equals being accepted', and when that was challenged he became petulant. His attitude and behaviour was damaging his relationship with both his father and brother, as well as causing hurt within himself. What angst we cause ourselves when we allow our internal rules to control our lives. When things don't work out well for us, what do our inner voices say? 'I don't try hard enough'? 'I must keep going'? 'I shouldn't do that'? 'Someone else would have done it better'? If we have problems with self-acceptance, we might say 'I'm rubbish', 'I'm stupid', 'I don't deserve anything good'. Let's remind ourselves of the father's words: 'My son... you are always with me, and everything I have is yours.'

Father, You have given me everything I need to live a life free from the need to prove myself to You. Help me to align my internal script with Your thoughts about me. Amen.

Capture those thoughts

READ: 2 CORINTHIANS 10:1–5

'we take captive every thought to make it obedient to Christ.' (v5)

We are considering the concept of internal scripts and rules that we apply to ourselves because of a belief system we have grown up with. They have also been described as an internal critical parent as opposed to an internal nurturing parent. Criticism can shut us down; nurturing can open us up. If our inner voice is more critical than nurturing, we will close ourselves off to the abundant life Jesus died to give us. That is not how our loving Father wants us to live.

Because we long to be accepted and feel valued, we generally behave in ways that we think will get us what we need. We are thirsty for a sense of worth from others, from what we do, from how we look, from how we behave. We were created to be loved and we may seek that love in many different ways. CWR founder Selwyn Hughes acknowledged that his success in writing gave him a real sense of satisfaction to the point that he began to depend on it. He said:

'I was drinking from a leaky cistern. I saw myself as a consummate professional rather than a desperately needy servant dependent on God alone for my soul's satisfaction. There and then I confessed my sin of misplaced dependency to the Lord, received His forgiveness, and rose to a new sense of commission'.[6] There was nothing wrong in Selwyn enjoying his writing and knowing the impact it had on others; it was his thinking that had become distorted, because he believed it was this and not God alone that gave him value and worth.

We too can drink from leaky cisterns (see Jer. 2:13), and when we are not satisfied, our thinking can lead to negative self-talk. But we have a way through this. Let's firstly recognise what we are thinking and decide to change that script. Secondly, let's confess it to God and ask for His forgiveness. Thirdly, let's accept His forgiveness and begin to change the narrative by taking those thoughts captive and coming into agreement with what God says about us.

Precious Lord, thank You that Your love for me is all I need to feel accepted. Help me to take any foolish thoughts captive and make them obedient to Christ. Amen.

● 20

Peace of mind

READ: PHILIPPIANS 4:8–9

'And the God of peace will be with you.' (v9)

Changing our thinking, and taking every thought captive, means we have something to do in order to co-operate with what the Holy Spirit wants to do in us, so that we can begin to accept ourselves as we are accepted by Him. Let's have today's verses in mind as we meditate on what to think about:

'Finally, brothers and sisters, whatever is true, whatever is noble, whatever is right, whatever is pure, whatever is lovely, whatever is admirable – if anything is excellent or praiseworthy – think about such things. Whatever you have learned or received or heard from me or seen in me – put it into practice. And the God of peace will be with you.' It's helpful to break this down.

'Whatever is true': Some of the words we tell ourselves are simply not true, they are lies. The enemy wants us to believe those lies but God wants us to know the truth. Saying 'I'm stupid', 'I'm worthless' or 'I'll never make it' are all statements that will keep us in a place of being ineffectual – and that's just what the enemy desires. God wants us to rise up and fly like eagles, working with Him to bless others.

'Whatever is noble': When we focus on honourable and kind thinking and behaviour it will be satisfying and pleasurable for our inner being and for others we spend time with.

'Whatever is right, pure and lovely': As you rest at night, think back on what has been good about the day, or how good Jesus is, and be thankful.

'Whatever is admirable, excellent and praiseworthy': We have so many things to praise God for. Consider some of the things you see, such as the kindness of others, or the creativity of God in nature. Thankfulness is like a comfort to the soul – it does us good.

Peace is the amazing gift we receive if we change our thinking, accept ourselves for who we are and live with thankfulness. Peace of mind brings a contentedness that striving for the world's approval will never achieve. Recognising that we are not perfect, and that we will not always get it right, releases us and builds a peaceful mind. This is a gift I want to possess, so I will definitely be reflecting on these words of Paul. Will you?

Dear Lord, as I contemplate these words, please feed my mind, soul and body with Your peace. Amen.

True to self

READ: ESTHER 2:15–19

'When the turn came for Esther… to go to the king, she asked for nothing other than what Hegai, the king's eunuch who was in charge of the harem, suggested.' (v15)

Esther's is an amazing story of courage, obedience and self-acceptance. This young woman was taken into a completely alien situation, far out of her comfort zone, and was now co-operating at the palace with those who were in charge of the harem. Esther had found favour with Hegai – he was impressed by her. We can imagine that she quietly did what was asked of her, accepting her situation without causing difficulty. Her demeanour found favour with the king and he chose her for his queen in the place of Vashti, who had angered him.

Living in a foreign country with different values from her Jewish heritage, Esther would have observed distinctions, but in the palace, she would have had to compromise her own traditions. The impressive thing is that she did not compromise her values. She remained loyal to Mordecai, she did not have to put herself in danger by revealing her nationality, and she maintained her integrity as a faithful Jewish woman.

Esther could so easily have allowed her thinking to take her down a road of self-pitying, fractious behaviour. Instead, her positive attitude and courageous spirit led to a Jewish victory in the face of their enemies. Mordecai's famous words, 'who knows but that you have come to your royal position for such a time as this?' (Esth. 4:14) ring down through the ages as a reminder that God has a plan for each of us – and Esther fulfilled her part in that plan, even though it could have cost her her life.

Self-acceptance, in the face of such challenges, is a powerful characteristic. Esther's skill in fulfilling Mordecai's direction and persuading the king was masterful, clever and well judged. As we learn to accept ourselves, we can approach difficult situations with integrity and confidence, and make considered decisions without having to be something we are not. As I write this, I am encouraged to consider how much more effective I can be in my life's work with an attitude like Esther's.

Lord, help me to embrace self-acceptance to the degree that it enables me to be more effective in life. Amen.

22

Do not worry!

READ: MATTHEW 6:25–34

'Therefore do not worry about tomorrow, for tomorrow will worry about itself. Each day has enough trouble of its own.' (v34)

Do you find yourself worrying about lots of things going on in your life right now? Then you might find today's title and verse laughable, saying, 'That's easy for you to say, but you haven't got my life or my situation!' But my question to you is: do you want to stay in that place of worry and let it dictate how you spend your day and your thoughts? What if we can find ways of dealing with those worrying thoughts so we are not hampered or brought down by them?

Trying to push worrying thoughts away may distract us for a while, but they are still there and can still have a negative impact on us. When we have troubling thoughts and emotions, it might help to stand back from them and view them from a different perspective. This can give us time to try to understand what is going on in our inner world. It's about being kind to that part of our inner being; protecting our mind and letting it rest from what might become toxic thinking. Stepping back and observing our thoughts gives us space to consider rather than immediately react.

The Message puts today's verse this way: 'Give your entire attention to what God is doing right now, and don't get worked up about what may or may not happen tomorrow. God will help you deal with whatever hard things come up when the time comes.' The key here is that God will help us. 1 Peter 5:6–7 says, 'Cast all your anxiety on him because he cares for you.' In order to cast our cares on Him, we have to acknowledge them, share them and let them go. Remember: He cares for us.

Self-acceptance recognises that in this life we will have disquieting thoughts and emotions, but we also have the ability to choose to change and let go of inner thoughts that can be so debilitating. So stand back, observe those thoughts, bring them before God, decide to leave them there, and move forward.

Lord, why am I discouraged? Why is my heart so sad? I will put my hope in You, God! I will praise You again, my Saviour and my God! Amen. (Based on Psa. 42:11)

23

Time to think

READ: JOHN 8:1–11

'But Jesus bent down and started to write on the ground with his finger.' (v6)

This story perfectly illustrates the judging tendency of negative thinking, the need to give ourselves time to consider, the kindness and forgiving nature of God, and the power of walking away and choosing to leave certain thoughts and behaviours behind.

Jesus had been teaching those who were hungry to experience His life-changing word. Then came the challenge from the Pharisees, who were determined to trip Him up. They wanted to trap Him and accuse Him of abusing the law. We don't know what Jesus wrote in the ground, but what we do know is that He gave Himself time to think. The challenges the Pharisees brought are like that inner critical voice and those worrying thoughts. Our minds can be so full of them and they can keep coming like the ceaseless barrage of questions for Jesus. What He said would have an impact on the questioners, the people who were being taught and, most crucially, the woman who was accused of adultery. It was life or death for her.

His response had to be thought through.

Perhaps He used this time to pray and be inspired by the Holy Spirit, as well as to step back and consider their accusations, the fact that the woman had broken the law, and the importance of His response. The truth is, Jesus cared for everyone present in that situation; His love wasn't and isn't conditional. The insistent accusers and the guilty woman all needed to experience His healing love. So He did something remarkable: He got the accusers to acknowledge their faults in their own hearts. In doing this, Jesus released the Pharisees from spiteful behaviour and the woman from her sins.

We can be thriving in our gifting and ministry, then suddenly be challenged by intrusive questioning and inner thoughts trying to trap us. Taking time to bring these things before God will enable us to look at them from His perspective. He will lovingly guide us through. Jesus didn't deny the woman's guilt, but He didn't condemn her either. His way is to forgive and encourage us to choose a new path forward.

Lord Jesus, thank You that You take time to listen to what is going on in my life, and gently encourage me to walk away from the negative and into Your abundant life. Amen.

24

Trust and rest

READ: ISAIAH 30:15–16

'In repentance and rest is your salvation, in quietness and trust is your strength, but you would have none of it.' (v15)

The Israelites had become independent of God in their thinking and in their behaviour. God said they were obstinate, rebellious, deceitful and unwilling to listen to Him. They only wanted to hear and experience pleasant and wonderful things; they didn't want to be confronted by the truth. This independence from God actually led them in the opposite direction – into dissatisfaction and inner turmoil.

God knows that when we come to Him in honesty, telling Him what is going on in our lives and receiving His rest and peace, we will experience salvation, which is about recovery from those things that would seek to hurt our souls. He wants us to be aware of His very great and powerful ability to restore us as we trust in Him and listen to His ways. But, He declares, the people were having none of it.

What about us? Surely salvation and strength are attributes we want to possess? I know I would.

And yet I also know that unless I am walking in the light of God's presence, I can so easily let the cares of this world, its lies and desires overwhelm me and cause a restless and perhaps fearful spirit within.

When Moses spoke with the Lord in the tent of meeting, He needed to know that God's presence was with him. His role of leading the Israelites was a challenging and problematic one, and he also knew they had many enemies. God said, 'My Presence will go with you, and I will give you rest' (Exod. 33:14). What a wonderful promise. Moses was so reliant on God's presence he immediately responded with, 'If your Presence does not go with us, do not send us up from here' (Exod. 33:15). You can hear the depth of his desire to know and experience the presence of God, as it distinguishes and characterises the lives of those who trust in Him.

As we spend time in God's loving presence, we will learn to be more at ease within our own hearts and minds, reflecting something of His strength and restful character. That sounds like a good place to be.

Father God, may Your presence be in my thinking, speaking and behaviour today and every day. Amen.

25

Living compassionately

READ: COLOSSIANS 3:12–15

'Therefore, as God's chosen people, holy and dearly loved, clothe yourselves with compassion, kindness, humility, gentleness and patience.' (v12)

The UK's Lake District is one of the most beautiful places I have ever been to. It goes without saying that there is a lot of water in the Lakes, and there is a lot of rain! There's no getting away from it: in order to enjoy and experience the beauty, you have to often endure the rain. Someone once said, 'There is no bad weather, only inappropriate clothing.' To make the most out of visiting the Lakes, and physically look after yourself, you have to have the right equipment, footwear and clothing.

But do we consider the 'clothing' we put on to care for ourselves emotionally? We often use today's verses to encourage us to live in harmony with one another, and, as we are told to love others as we love ourselves, we can surely apply these words to our inner being. Importantly, as we develop a compassionate and caring attitude towards ourselves, we find that we feel more at ease, and therefore rested emotionally and physically.

Self-compassion is about having a healthy respect for ourselves by being kind to our own heart and mind, despite our inadequacies and weaknesses. It is an essential part of our wellbeing. Compassion and empathy towards others is the ability to try to see things from their perspective, reaching out a hand to help them see they have significance and worth, and supporting them through their journey. Do you feel you are valuable enough to give that support to yourself? Jesus clearly does. He said, 'Come to me, all you who are weary and burdened, and I will give you rest. Take my yoke upon you and learn from me, for I am gentle and humble in heart, and you will find rest for your souls. For my yoke is easy and my burden is light' (Matt. 11:28–30).

Do we carry the burden of low self-esteem, being hard on ourselves and finding it difficult to receive blessings from God and others? This is not Jesus' will for our lives. Let's come into agreement with Him and receive His compassion and kindness by being compassionate and kind towards ourselves.

Lord, teach me to receive Your compassion and rest. Help me to learn to be compassionate towards myself. Amen.

26

God showers us with compassion

READ: PSALM 145:8–20

'The LORD is merciful and compassionate, slow to get angry and filled with unfailing love.' (v8, NLT)

Having been created in the image of God, we bear His characteristics. Therefore we have the capacity to be compassionate. Meditating on this quality will help us to foster it within ourselves. In fact, focusing on the goodness of God's attributes in general will enhance our understanding of Him and allow us recognise the ways in which we can reflect them in our own lives. As we spend time in His presence, we can gradually become transformed into His likeness. New and transforming thoughts will increase our self-acceptance and help us to understand that as redeemed children of the King, we can grow in maturity towards spiritual health and wellbeing. What a privilege.

What else does this psalm say about who God is? He is good, majestic and glorious, keeps His promises and is gracious, helps the fallen, satisfies hunger and thirst, is righteous and kind, is close by, hears our cries for help, and protects. Wow! What an amazing Father we have. When I read those words, I ask myself how I could possibly stay in a place of low self-worth or lacking in self-acceptance. Because this Father wants to nurture me into the fullness of life, lacking no good thing, it wouldn't make sense to live feeling worthless and not accepting myself with my imperfections! And though I often *am* in a place of deep contentment and assurance, there are times I find that I need to come back to this truth and remind myself of the joy of living loved – unconditionally.

Our trek through life can be threatened or enhanced by our ability to accept ourselves where we are, knowing we will grow in faith, maturity, trust and the likeness of our creator. Spending time with Him – considering our relationship with Him, what He has done and is doing for us – will take us closer towards being men and women who have self-compassion. From this place we can reach out to others more completely and even more honestly.

Father, thank You that You have not held back from declaring Your love and compassion for me. Help me to live in that and to honour You by loving others. Amen.

27

We are blessed

READ: EPHESIANS 1:1–14

'Even before he made the world, God loved us and chose us in Christ to be holy and without fault in his eyes.' (v4, NLT)

As we come towards the end of our readings on self-acceptance, this is a truly inspiring passage to consider. Paul wrote this letter to the Christians in Ephesus to encourage them to think of themselves differently. They had previously been led by idol worship and bad theology, causing them to live unhealthily. Paul encouraged them to discover their new identity 'in Christ' – a phrase he uses 28 times in this letter alone. Not only do these words give a clear picture of how magnificent God is and what He has done for us, but they show an astonishing insight into how Paul's life had been changed. This man, formerly bent on destroying the Church had been utterly transformed and captured by Jesus to the point that he can encourage us in this way still today. So, we remind ourselves that if Paul can experience such a radical transformation in his thinking, perspective and attitude, then so can you and I.

Paul tells us we are 'united with Christ' and that we are chosen 'in Christ to be holy and without fault in his eyes' (vv3–4, NLT). How wonderful! The importance of our relationship with God is defined by the fact that Jesus shed His blood for us so we can walk in freedom. Our inheritance, because we are His children, is that we are in family relationship with Him and will be for ever. We are invited to live in this place of privilege, freedom and relationship, without having to do a thing. It is a gift. But if we truly want to receive this gift, we need to accept what it means and let it profoundly affect our sense of identity in Christ, as it did for Paul.

Paul's change was extreme and immediate, wheras our pattern of change may be slower and gentler. In either case, letting the Spirit of God into our lives with a desire for a shift in how we see our identity will certainly bear good fruit. The more we understand who we are in Christ, the less powerful that inner critical voice will become. Acknowledging our place in God's kingdom will increase our ability to love and accept ourselves as He does.

Lord, help me to absorb the truth that I have read in Your Word. Let it transform my sense of identity, so I truly accept I am Your child and heir. Amen.

28

Abundantly free

READ: EPHESIANS 1:3–14

'So we praise God for the glorious grace he has poured out on us who belong to his dear Son.' (v6)

We reflect on these verses again as a wonderful promise that we have been adopted into the most incredible family, with all of its heritage and privileges. Our heavenly Father does not hold back on what He offers, nor does He neglect to fulfil His promises. One of the most important lessons I have learned over the years is that the more time I spend reading and reflecting on the Scriptures, the more powerfully they affect my life. This includes discovering what God says about Himself and His relationship with me. I find those words affecting my lifestyle, my heart and my mind, and my spirit. They are life-giving and life-changing. Hebrews 4:12 says, 'For the word of God is alive and active. Sharper than any double-edged sword, it penetrates even to dividing soul and spirit, joints and marrow; it judges the thoughts and attitudes of the heart.' I personally have found that to be so true.

Very often I believe I hear God speaking to me through the promises, declarations and affirming words I read in the Bible. This is what I hear from today's verses:

I am your Father and I will bless you with every blessing because you are part of my family. I knew you before time began, you are my chosen child, and I have such joy in receiving you into my heart. I have so much I want to give you. I want to pour out my grace and kindness towards you in abundance, along with wisdom and understanding. My forgiveness towards you is complete.

I have a plan to bring all things under the authority of my Son. You have an inheritance and so are part of that plan. I have already identified you as my own. I have saved you through my Son. My Holy Spirit, who lives in you, is the guarantee that you will receive everything I have for you.

Father, thank You that I am part of Your family, that You want to pour out Your blessings on me. As I reflect on the truth I've found in Your Word today, may it sink into my spirit, my mind and my heart, bringing me to a place of assurance that I am truly loved by You. Amen.

29

Be transformed

READ: ROMANS 12:1–13

'Do not conform to the pattern of this world, but be transformed by the renewing of your mind.' (v2)

We began this devotional by looking at how we can so easily compare ourselves to others and, in our minds, come off second best. We can also be influenced by what we consider others might be thinking about us, our personal beliefs and our mistakes or failures. Having looked at the truth in God's Word and discovered what He thinks about us, and knowing that whatever we have done in the past is forgiven when we come to Him, we can begin to experience a transformation. And it begins in the mind.

When we look at God, He wants us to see Him as one who loves us endlessly, is forgiving and compassionate, accepts us as we are and patiently and gently moves us into all He knows we can be. And though it's important not to be arrogant or proud, verse 3 says, 'Be honest in your evaluation of yourselves' (NLT). God has clearly given each one of us gifts and abilities, some of which are mentioned here, which we are to use willingly for His glory. It is a huge joy and privilege to use our God-given talents to bless and encourage others – let's remember that. If our lack of self-acceptance holds us back, we may miss the incredible journey He wants to take us on right now.

Knowing who we are in Jesus – accepting our destiny and identity as children of the King of kings – helps to create within us a feeling of worth. We need to learn to abandon the belief we may have had of ourselves as unlovable or having no purpose and being worthless – that is not who we are. God powerfully draws us to Himself through the sacrifice of His Son and the daily encouragement of the Holy Spirit. We are no longer defined by our past or present circumstances but by what God thinks about us.

We are His masterpiece (Eph. 2:10), the apple of His eye (Psa. 17:8), His own (2 Cor. 1:22), complete in Him (Col. 2:10). Not only that: 'God raised us up with Christ and seated us with him in the heavenly realms in Christ Jesus' (Eph. 2:6). Though our feet are on the ground, our spiritual lives are lived from a heavenly perspective. You have been raised to that place. How amazing!

Lord, I pray that I will fully accept my position in You, knowing I am loved, accepted and wanted. Amen.

30

He speaks peace

READ: JOHN 14:23–27

'Peace I leave with you; my peace I
give you.' (v27)

On our last day pondering the concept of self-
acceptance, we could end in no better way than
reflecting on the gift Jesus gave His disciples
before His crucifixion, as told in this verse. Jesus
knew His friends would face problems because
of their faith, and that this would challenge their
emotional as well as their physical wellbeing.
These words resound through the ages because
they are words of comfort and assurance for all
people. Jesus knows we all need the gift of peace
in our lives – the kind of peace that overcomes
trouble and fear.

In Psalm 85, the psalmist describes the
blessings God has poured out on His people
and recognises that they needed to be restored
again after times of great trouble. That is so like
us, isn't it? We can go along being confident of
who we are in Jesus, assured of our identity, and
then, often when we face difficulties, we become
independent of God again and need reviving.
Let's remind ourselves of the big-heartedness

of our loving God. He restores, forgives, loves, saves, promises peace and gives what is good. God is faithful and righteous, and that means we can totally depend on Him because He cannot go against His character. Bound up in His attributes of faithfulness and righteousness are love and peace. And we get it all! Nothing is held back.

As we experience growth in our ability to accept ourselves for who we are in Jesus, we get all His mighty strength to help us and all His Father's heart to guide us. What an incredible place to be. May we put ourselves into His safe hands, trusting that our self-acceptance will become well-balanced and assured.

Father, thank You that Your faithful love and righteous heart accepts me for who I am. You created me, enabled me, saved me and You love me with an unconditional love. Help me to receive Your peace so that, whenever I face the kind of challenges that could rob me of my confidence, I may find comfort in the knowledge that You are always there with me. Amen.

ENDNOTES

[1] Isabelle Myers Briggs and Peter B. Myers, *Gifts Differing: Understanding Personality Type* (Palo Alto, CA: CPP Books, 1993) p54.
The Myers-Briggs Type indicator can be a really helpful for people on a journey of self-acceptance and self-understanding. We occasionally run teaching days on this at Waverley Abbey House. For more information, visit cwr.org.uk/courses

[2] Max Lucado, *Cure for the Common Life* (Nashville, TN: Thomas Nelson, 2005) p55

[3] 'Collected letters of CS Lewis Vol III © copyright CS Lewis Pte Ltd 2006.' Used with permission.

[4] You can find out more about the Inner Critical Voice in Chapter 3 of *An Insight into Self-Acceptance* by Chris Ledger and Claire Musters.

[5] You can find out more about Internal Scripts in Chapter 4 of *An Insight into Self-Acceptance* by Chris Ledger and Claire Musters.

[6] Selwyn Hughes, *Christ Empowered Living* (Farnham: CWR, 2002) pp113–114

Discover the full Insight range

Discover our full range of Insight resources and courses, all of which provide accessible and practical insights on tough issues that so many of us face in our lives today. The series has been developed to help people understand and work through these key issues, drawing on real-life case studies, biblical examples and counselling practices. Whether for yourself or to help support someone you know, we have one-off Insight books, courses and daily devotionals on key topics. Find out more at **cwr.org.uk/insight**

These Three Things:
Finding your Security,
Self-worth and Significance

How do you sum up, in one book, content that covers our deep spiritual needs, personal motivations, and revival? Homesickness and belonging? Our disconnection, isolation and reconnection with God and others in our increasingly 'contactless' society? Let's start by going back to the original plan: who God is, and who we are; where it all went wrong, and how we find our way back; what it is we're looking for, and how and where to find it; all while daring to ask the questions:

- Who am I?
- Do I matter?
- What's the point?

Find out more and
order at **cwr.org.uk/ttt**

Free online resources available for groups and churches

There's something for everyone!

Find God in your everyday

If you love to spend time with God, then why not take ten extra minutes to hear from God and understand His Word? CWR's range of Bible reading notes include something for everyone, including *Every Day with Jesus*, *Inspiring Women Every Day*, and Jeff Lucas' *Life Every Day*.

Find out more at **cwr.org.uk/store**

Courses and seminars

Waverley Abbey College

Publishing and media

Conference facilities

Transforming lives

CWR's vision is to enable people to experience personal transformation through applying God's Word to their lives and relationships.

Our Bible-based training and resources help people around the world to:

- Grow in their walk with God
- Understand and apply Scripture to their lives
- Resource themselves and their church
- Develop pastoral care and counselling skills
- Train for leadership
- Strengthen relationships, marriage and family life and much more.

CWR Applying God's Word to everyday life and relationships

CWR, Waverley Abbey House,
Waverley Lane, Farnham,
Surrey GU9 8EP, UK

Telephone: +44 (0)1252 784700
Email: info@cwr.org.uk
Website: cwr.org.uk

Registered Charity No. 294387
Company Registration No. 1990308

Our insightful writers provide daily Bible reading notes and other resources for all ages, and our experienced course designers and presenters have gained an international reputation for excellence and effectiveness.

CWR's Training and Conference Centre in Surrey, England, provides excellent facilities in idyllic settings - ideal for both learning and spiritual refreshment.